THE
STARS
WITH
YOU

Cooper
Dillon

THE STARS WITH YOU

STEFANI COX

The Stars With You
Copyright © 2022 by Stefani Cox
All rights reserved. First edition.

Cooper Dillon Books
San Diego, California
CooperDillon.com

Cover Design & Interior by Adam Deutsch
Author image by EricJ

ISBN-13: 978-1943899-15-9

Table of Contents

Thorns	1
Zora knew	2
Inherited 1	4
Inherited 2	5
Storm Borne	6
Ward	7
Lessons	8
Make it through the night	9
No need for counting sheep.	10
Where Is There	11
Voice of The Undead	13
Body Memory	14
That Tenth	15
Sliding Stories	16
Modern Potions	17
I Am The Ritual	18
Company	19
On Divinity	20
Vertigo	21
Refuge	22
She will mine	23
Notice	24
Apocalypse Litany	25

"I have been in Sorrow's kitchen and licked out all the pots. Then I have stood on the peaky mountain wrapped in rainbows, with a harp and a sword in my hands."

-Zora Neale Hurston, *Dust Tracks on a Road,* 1942.

Thorns

She didn't choose her garden
the one she started with
weed bloom choke
searching sun.

Her field is a cluster of lilacs and storm water
petunias mired in bramble—

she can't figure out what to do about the bramble.

Love your dark.

She tries
waters best she can—
still
some seasons
envelop.

She fears she
can't manage
all the parcels.

Where are her plow and mule?

Zora knew

being crazy
is a Black woman's freedom

saw every
damn day is like
a request line for

—your body
—its labor
—held wisdom
—hope
—ambitions

somebody please
hang up the call

with so much desire
coming hard as
flash rains after lightning

the floods they make

you understand why
the mind slips
(a little)
now and again

spirits step up
to my whirlpool

some
pull me out
others
push me deeper in

I dance awhile
cloaked in mist
wrapped in
cloud smoke

turn circles
find reflection
lost and stationed
all the same

Inherited 1

Who can-cans down
the shoulders of my relatives,
dirty feet pressing firm?

Needed because

they

they
are always watching
waiting to confirm
minstrel nature
fried chicken gnawing
habits and
ash everywhere.

Save a life or ruin it.

My head
is stuffed with threats
my head a zoo.

Inherited 2

I box strong
as my ancestors
punches well-learned
bequeathed moves
except

now a glance
means a thought
means a latent potential

for action against
this body-mind
this heart.

Uppercut
no match for a
bump in the night
that only has meaning
to me.

Storm Borne

Patterns always
       find me first

There's chaff

and then
that's me

a s k e w
&   twirling

like when
     drag lines
          catch a current

Ward

Blackness
    ~~is a~~
    has a
    weight

trauma a certain number
of pounds.

Ancestors way back
took dimensions
heft height length.

They watched over
they protected
because anguish needs
a caretaker.

Feed.
Keep hands
from mouth.
Touch arms

loving
tender.

I follow instructions
best I can
which means
not quite so good
after all.

Lessons

ghosts surf
her body
    no
body drafts
in wake
while ghosts
will k no w
      no
        body

a ghost is
not a body
ghost has
  no   body
body surfs
in wake
is wake
awake

her body

never learned
to swim

Make it through the night

tremors

mind latching to
next   and next
and next

until
panic bursts free
   spreads like
cancer or plague

stress and free radicals.
I know it's

twice as bad for the cells
to be   twice as good

innards are subject
   to swiping
hashing
   to bits

and being spat on.

I will not be
invitation to arrows.

No need for counting sheep.

We don't sleep anyway,
we built the world from our exhaustion.

An old woman inhabits this body—
Black don't crack, but DNA does,
its ability to phoenix degraded every day.

So keep your cows and fluffy animals
for the other kind of life, where our diligence
is lofted and our hands will meet the earth.

I doze, I wake, such vivid dreams
can only be my wish.

Where Is There

Home
is not a place
Home
was a place   torn
from my grandmother's father's
father's mother

Home is not somewhere
I can point to on a map

I don't know
how to talk to
friends with homes
a country or two to show off

Home is where the

Home is a fleeting idea
urban butterfly lost to smog

Hold on so the mental tear
grows smaller
the more you
buy
the more you
keep
the more you
claim

in a world that
has only ever
taken away

we build home
make home this way
so as not to be

packable tent
spirits
setting up shop
like the carnival

just as easily gone

Voice of The Undead

she doesn't feel like a whole person.
she feels like a bunch of other people
crammed into one body.

she is older than you know.
she is deep mama running clean.
she is loud and boisterous before
she falls into silence.

we hate the way you look at her
when you threaten to call her crazy.

Body Memory

My brain lacks

needs infusion
to stop
tiny willful
chemicals from
reabsorption
and imbalance.

We were the experiment once
pieces of sinew + cell
for the microscope.

Two serpents
love a cross
answer questions
that our bodies pose—

am I foolish
to trust again?

That Tenth

My mind costs $_ _ _ , _ _ _
plus assorted expenses and fees

all that worth capped and bottled
between my ears above shoulders

top heavy means ready to fall

but
with a mind you can duel up
the white man.

My predecessors
they fought and

this is how they won.

Only now

I've lost my body
I've lost my organs
and all

food is a mechanism
for brain power
just

another payment
for the ledger.

Sliding Stories

There are more than
gods and monsters
ancestors and spirit
company
they keep

Who navigates
the space
between this breath
and then the next?

An agent has a name
a name
the one who
takes her down

but not until you
guard an angel

catch a tail
   and hold it tight

Modern Potions

We don't need
no cauldrons
we bite this earth
to taste its silt

invocation
or prayer
we make a
way
we lift our own.

I write for all
us Black girl witches
even if we didn't
learn from mama

create a
sourcebook
among sisters

we raise energy
our hands
and harried limbs
each downward dog
a metaphor

tea leaves
and herb gardens
tarot and late night
chocolate
water drunk
and released
down cheeks

rituals to hold a generation
women to hold our truths.

I Am The Ritual

Pour water
light candle
smudge altar
and scent of
lavender bloom.

Lay card across
my stomach
and sigh shore
    closer
anoint again.

Company

I run with
energies
I hold no
candle to

spirits
and their
spirits' spirits
play me
like putty

thrumming
high and tight

I endeavor
to keep them
all in check

unruly to
polite and
yet

I worry
one day
they'll eat me
out of house
and home

wash me down
with a gulp of water.

On Divinity

I talk about gods
as if   I know them
arriving here from where
the   elephants move

as if one morning
   I'll wake up
to spirits   bouncing
   off the windowpane

they'll act as if
   they own the place
and I'll   lie still

bathed in magic

properly
struck with awe.

Vertigo

I can't hold all
my freedom at once
can't fathom the choices
my great-grandmother
never had

that fall before
my feet like jewels
glitter with
the hope of every single
Black dream.

I can't hold all
my freedom at once
and some nights
I can't hold any
because

it just makes me
too dizzy.

Refuge

Could we drop it here
where
cut grass
blends

mixes
freshness with
sweat of passers-by?

The stone
might knock
a small brown bird

and yet
we'd let it fall.

Brush reveals
a different kind

shed skin
hiss of snakes

stormwaters
pepper
aged roots
a thirsty mole
prays thanks.

This tiny wind
the space it leaves
at junction of
us and earth.

She will mine

hunting and
sifting this dirt because she knows
we know
we know
all this leads to mulch.

Ancestors unfurled through the wings at her back
do you trust us to show you the way?

believe when we tell you shoveling is the answer

glittering remnants
a testament—
what it means to try.

*I miss it.
I miss being in the stars
with you.*

Apocalypse Litany

At the end of the world
   we are conscious
   we feel connection like
     a bone between the teeth
   we understand.

At the end of the world
   sit Ms. Morrison
   Ms. Butler
   Ms. Tubman and
   their kin, friends
   rediscovered
   as the buildings
   crash on down.

At the end of the world
   we have space
   each visit space
   live with arms
   widespread

past the bombs
   and the burnt
   out bits lies
   that pesky dream
   King reclined
   atop it.

At the end of the world.
At the end of the world.
At the end of the world.

Beliefs that
I need to shove on.

Stefani Cox is a poet and writer with an MFA from UC Riverside. Her work has been published in *The Rumpus, LeVar Burton Reads,* and *Lost Balloon,* among other outlets. Stefani has received fellowships to Hedgebrook, Tin House, Yefe Nof, and VONA. She has also served as an editor for *Santa Ana River Review, Speculative City,* and *PodCastle* magazines. Stefani lives in Los Angeles with her husband and a grumpy but lovable senior Chiweenie.

www.ingramcontent.com/pod-product-compliance
Lightning Source LLC
Chambersburg PA
CBHW030142100526
44592CB00011B/1009